Coin Hunting Made Easy

Finding Silver, Gold and Other Rare Valuable Coins for Profit and Fun

By Mark Smith

Coin Hunting Made Easy

ISBN-13: 978-1500992651
ISBN-10: 1500992658
Coin Hunting Made Easy: Finding Silver, Gold and Other Rare Valuable Coins for Profit and Fun

Table of Contents

Other Best Selling Books By the Author

Metal Detecting: A Beginner's Guide to Mastering the Greatest Hobby In the World

Finding treasure with a metal detector is real and doing it is simple and easy once you read this book. There are people finding incredible old coins made from gold and silver, valuable historical relics and old jewelry made from gold, silver and platinum. But you won't find these great treasures unless you know where and how to look. Metal Detecting: A Beginner's Guide shows you this and much more.

Veteran detectorist and treasure enthusiast Mark Smith continues to provide great information to anyone interested in the great hobby of metal detecting. In his second book on the subject, he manages to answer the common questions that every novice has when they are thinking about getting started. From choosing the right machine to identifying your valuable treasure, Mark Smith covers these subjects and everything in between in an easy to understand way.

Metal Detecting The Beach

Do you ever dream of finding buried treasures on the beach? Have you sat there and watched as other people comb the beach with their metal detectors wondering if they ever really find anything? Do you think that they would be there doing it if they were not finding anything? These people are digging up silver, gold, diamonds, platinum, old coins, and every other type of treasure that you could imagine. It is real. There is an entire world of buried treasure right beneath your feet, and it is waiting for you to dig it all up.

<u>Incredible Metal Detecting Discoveries: True Stories of Amazing Treasures Found by Everyday People</u>
Veteran detectorist, treasure enthusiast and best selling author Mark Smith continues to provide great information to anyone interested in the great hobby of metal detecting. In his third book on the subject, he showcases the best treasures unearthed using nothing more than a metal detector. Each true story of amazing treasure discoveries will have you itching to get out there and find your very own piece of treasure. From monster gold nuggets worth millions of dollars to ancient buried hoards that consist of thousands of gold coins, the stories in this book will take your breath away!

But this book contains much more than treasure stories. Each story teaches a valuable lesson that anyone can learn from. It doesn't matter if you are interested in metal detecting or not. These stories will fascinate anyone who has even the smallest interest in treasure and adventure.

Introduction

The experience of peeling away the paper from a roll of old coins and revealing a glint of silver or gold never gets old. When the light hits these coins, they produce an almost magical luster that is reflected in the eagerness of my eyes and the huge smile on my face.

It takes me back to those Christmas mornings when I was a kid and my brother and I tore through wrapping paper like little Tasmanian Devils. We knew there was something special underneath those layers of brightly colored paper, and our eager little hands could not remove the paper fast enough.

It is great to feel that way again as an adult, but instead of discovering bright and shiny toys under a layer of paper, I am discovering old and very valuable coins. Bringing my children along for this fun filled ride makes the entire experience even more gratifying.

I can't accurately describe in words how magical it is to see your child open a roll of coins and watch their little hands tremble with excitement. To see them at a loss of words as they try to grasp the reality of the current situation is worth every single penny of gas invested in the journey.

The look on their faces when they discover an entire roll of silver coins is absolutely priceless. My son now has a coin collection that rivals the Smithsonian Institution's National Numismatic Collection. Woah! That is a tongue twister. Say it three times fast. I bet you can't!

All joking aside, this is the reality of what some people have coined (pun intended) "coin roll hunting." There are millions of coins out there that hold a secret value. These coins could be simple pennies that you have sitting at the bottom of your sock drawer, or they could be a stack of silver dollars an elderly lady just brought to the bank. Knowing how and where to find these valuable coins is all part of the addictive fun.

Don't worry, I will openly share the best methods to this coin hunting madness. Get ready to dive head first into another addictive hobby that could be worth millions!

My First Experience Coin Roll Hunting

Coin roll hunting has a lot to do with luck and the odds are going to be stacked in your favor. You will eventually find something of value, but you never know what it is going to be. My first experience coin roll hunting proved this point.

I asked my son if he would like to try a new method of finding old coins. I told him we could make an entire day of it. We were already digging up old coins with the help of our trusty metal detector. Because of our metal detecting adventures, my son was already an avid coin collector. There was no matter of convincing him to go on what would later become an adventure of epic proportions.

We would scale the highest snow capped mountains never once fearing the Abominable Snowman. We would travel by mule through Death valley never once stopping for water. We would man a small submarine and travel to the bottom of the Mariana Trench never once fearing the mighty Kraken. Okay, we weren't really going to be doing any of these crazy things. We would just be driving around town in the comfort of our vehicle.

Our first stop was my very own bank. I needed some cash to play around with. I would be exchanging paper money for rolled coins. It was a very simple process.

The teller would become the only obstacle standing

between me and my coin hunting addiction. She or he had to feel compelled to help me. Some people can be easily persuaded with something as simple as a compliment. Others are an impenetrable wall of seething anger. There is nothing you can possibly do to persuade these people to help you. Don't waste your time.

I made a withdrawal of $100 in cash. I thought that would be enough to play around with, but I quickly learned I would need much more than that.

Before the teller handled my transaction, I noticed she was adjusting her hair in a small hand held mirror. Okay, it was time to turn on the smolder. I handed her my withdrawal slip without saying a single word. As she typed the information into her computer I said, "Your hair looks nice." This wasn't a lie. Her hair did look nice. She stopped typing and with a big smile she replied, "Thank you!"

Her smile didn't fade as she handed me my crisp pile of twenties and asked, "Is there anything else I can do for you?" I paused acting like there was nothing else I needed and then I said, "Oh yes there is, now that you mention it. Do you happen to have any half dollars? It doesn't matter if they are loose or rolled. My son likes to collect them," I said as he flashed her his pearly whites. Yes we were working as a team.

She paused for a second and said, "Oh yeah. Someone just brought in $50.00 worth. How many would you like?"

"We will take all of them!" I eagerly replied.

I handed her my cash and she handed me five rolls of half dollars. I couldn't believe how easy that was.

My son and I exited the bank and went to our car. I handed him the rolls and explained what we were looking for. Out of the 100 half dollars in our first batch, we found three dated 1964. These coins were 90% silver!

I know its not quite a jackpot, but we traveled less than 3 miles to find them. We were both amazed. My son looked at me and said, "Let's go to the next bank." I put the keys in the ignition and started the car.

We spent the entire day driving from bank to bank doing this same exact thing. At some banks we were lucky enough to find a few silver half dollars, at others we found nothing, but we were having a blast doing it.

At each new stop I would look over to my son and say, "This time you do the talking." His response was always the same. "No way! Dad."

Our time was almost up. The clock was quickly approaching 4:00 P.M. It wouldn't be long until the bank lobbies were closed. I looked at my son and said, "We have time to try one more bank."

We pulled into a Bank of America and patiently waited in a

very long line. I approached the teller and asked her if she had any half dollars rolled or loose. She happily replied, "Yes we do. How many do you need?"

I smiled and replied, "How many do you have?"

Her reply was not what I expected. She said, "$250.00 worth."

I only had $50.00 in my pocket. My mind was racing. Should I buy $250.00 worth of half dollars? That was a lot of money to sink into this little game my son and I were playing.

I told myself, "There is no loss. Just deposit the face value coins back into your bank account."

I told the teller to give me all of them and take it from the balance in my checking account. My son and I waited while the teller disappeared into the vault. She came back with an old shoe box full of hand rolled half dollars and slid them across the counter.

My eyes were about to pop out of my skull when I saw those old hand rolled coins. The paper was old, grimy and moldy in a few spots. These coins had been trapped in their little paper prisons for a very long time.

My hands trembled as I grabbed the old shoe box. I threw the teller a quick reassuring smile that said, "Yeah, I am all right. Just ignore the crazed look on my face for the moment."

The walk back to my car that day was very long. Time had slowed and I could feel my heart racing in my chest. I couldn't help it. I had $250.00 in half dollars in my hand and they were all hand rolled. These sort of things excite me.

When we got to the car, my son and I climbed into the back seat and stared at the huge pile of rolled coins in the shoebox. "Here ya go buddy. Tear into these suckers." I said pointing to the pile of coins.

It was Christmas morning all over again as my son tore through the rolled coins. The first few rolls were just regular Kennedy half dollars. Nothing special, but then my son tore into a roll and a coin fell into his hands.

The small grooves on the surface of the coin were filled with years of dirt and grime. He held the coin up and said, "What is this? I have never even seen one of these before."

It was a 1945 Walking Liberty Half dollar. I will be honest with you, I never once thought we would find something quite so old and valuable at our local bank, but what happened next almost made me poop my pants.

Two more Walking Liberty Half dollars popped out of the same roll. At this point my son's little hands were starting to tremble. I knew he was very excited, but I had to ask him, "What's wrong?" He was speechless, but the lucky streak wasn't about to end.

The old hand rolled halves continued to produce old silver coins. There were even a few silver mercury head dimes shoved in between the halves. We were both in complete and total shock.

By the time we were done, we had three Walking Liberty half dollars, six Franklin half dollars, 36 silver Kennedy half dollars, two silver mercury dimes and one 1986 Statue of Liberty Commemorative half dollar. I couldn't believe my eyes. Here's a picture we took that afternoon when we got home.

Yeah we hit the jackpot that day and it is something neither of us will ever forget. This was almost five years ago and my son and I have learned there are other valuable coins floating around out there in circulation. We now target all sorts of coins and we are eagerly snatching them up every single chance we get.

3 Facts About Valuable Coins In Today's Society

Spending countless hours metal detecting introduced me to an entire new world of valuable coins, coins that could be worth 10 times their face value or even more. I was eagerly digging up these valuable coins as often as I could find them.

I had what you could call a healthy appetite to find more, but there were times when I couldn't get outside in the great wide open. It could be that a few days of rain settled over my location, or it could be that the icy grip of winter buried all of my valuable coin targets under a blanket of ice and snow.

I needed to find another way to feed my hunger, and It didn't take me long to discover another fantastic way to increase my pile of valuable coins, and to think these coins were right under my nose the entire time!

When I first heard about this, I didn't believe it was possible, but I quickly learned otherwise. There are millions of extremely valuable coins that are in circulation right at this moment. You may even have some sitting in a jar, the center console of your vehicle or a drawer someplace in your home. This is **fact number one**.

Let me ask you a question. When was the last time you used some actual physical money to buy something? It might have been a while, right? Modern technology has all but eliminated physical currency. People are getting paid electronically and they are spending their money electronically too. This is **fact number two**. I do it and just about everyone I know does it as well. It is just the way things are. This left one burning question in my mind.

Where did all the actual physical money go?
Think about that for a minute. In the United States alone there have been billions of coins created. If everyone is using electronic methods to pay for everything, where did all of these coins go? They all probably ended up in a bank somewhere right?

Ahh. This was the moment the light bulb went off in my head. Banks have vaults and I bet they are full of physical currency. This made perfect sense to me, and then I remembered what my grandparents did with their change. They just tossed it all into one of those gigantic old five gallon water jugs. They never took the time to look through it.

The truth is a good percentage of the general public does not know a thing about valuable coins. They are far too busy in their day to day lives to stop and look at the value associated with a simple coin. To them it is just an old coin. This is **fact number three** and a fact the would be coin collector like myself can easily capitalize on and so can you. Let's go find some valuable coins.

Learning the Lingo

Every hobby seems to come with its own lingo and coin roll hunting is no different. In fact, the entire world of coin collecting has its own dictionary. I will be using a few terms in this book that you may not be all that familiar with. I may have already done this. (sorry about that)

Learning the lingo in regards to coin collecting can help you increase your pile of collectible coins. Many of the oddities that you may want to target have unique names that you don't hear every day on the street, in the office or at the local pub.

The following terms are the most common terms used throughout this book and coin roll hunting in general.

Reading the following section is not by any means a requirement, especially if you consider yourself to be a coin collecting linguistics major, but if you think Double Die is the name of the next James Bond movie, then you might want to continue reading. Knowledge is power they say!

Bag Marks

Carrying around a large amount of coins is not easy. These things can get quite heavy. In order to make things easier, coins are transported in large bags. While they are loose in a bag, they may come into contact with other coins. Small nicks and blemishes can occur. These are called bag marks.

Bullion

Bullion is a term related to precious metals that are pure or very close to it. There are silver, gold and platinum bullion coins made specifically for collecting precious metals or for investing purposes. These coins do not generally have a face value, and they are usually sold in one ounce increments. Finding a bullion coin while coin roll hunting is like winning the coin roll hunting lottery!

Circulated Coins

These are coins that have been in use by the general public. They will have nicks, scuff marks and other minor flaws that have a direct impact on the value of the coin.

Clad

Clad is any modern money that is made from non-precious metals. The majority of coins in circulation are clad. We don't want these, unless of course they have errors.

Commemorative Coin

These are special coins that are not generally used for circulation, but you can and will find them while coin roll hunting. These coins have been created to commemorate a special time, place or event.

Denomination

This is the actual face value of an intended coin. A quarter has a face value of 25 cents.

Die

This is what happens when I play video games. I die. It is because of this that I have decided to stop. Just kidding of course.

A die is what is used to make the fancy designs we see on coins. You could think of the die as the mold for a coin. Most common error coins are a result of a broken or malfunctioning die.

Edge

The side of a coin that runs the entire circumference. This is often confused with rim.

Error

The United States Mint occasionally makes errors when they manufacture coins. These error coins can be worth more than their intended face value and sometimes they show up in coin rolls. See chapter titled: **What To Look For**

Face Value

See Denomination above.

Grade or Grading

The practice of assigning a Grade to a coin for the sole means of determining a value. This is one grading system where the letter "F" is not something to be ashamed of.

Halves

Another word for half dollars. These are the best place to start looking for some silver.

Keeper
Any coin that you have decided to keep. It could be a penny with a hole in it, or it could be a $5.00 Liberty Head gold coin.

Key Date
Key date coins are coins which are considered rare for any number of reasons. It could be that very few were created, or it could be a date when an error occurred.

Loupe
This is a special hand held magnifying glass that jewelers use to get up close and personal with stones. A loupe will make finding common errors, mint marks and other coin oddities much easier.

Melt Value
A perfectly cooked pizza loaded with fresh veggies has a melt value of 10. That reminds me, I never ate lunch.

Melt value in the coin world refers to the current value of the precious metal a coin is made from. For instance, a 1964 Kennedy half dollar is 90% silver. The current market value or spot price of silver would be considered the melt value of the coin.

I am not suggesting you melt down any of your coins. In

fact, melting certain coins is against the law in the United States.

Mint Mark
See the chapter titled: Understanding Mint Marks

Numismatics
This is the complicated to spell and pronounce word that has been chosen to represent the collecting of any type of currency. Couldn't they have picked a better word for this?

Numismatic Value
This is much different than melt value because it pertains to coins that have a high value regardless of precious metal content. For instance, the 1909 VDB penny has an extremely high numismatic value because it features the initials of the wheat penny designer prominently displayed on the back.

The general public loved the new coin design, but they complained about the designer's initials being so predominant. The initials were removed but not until after over 480,000 of the coins were minted.

The VDB penny is one of the rarest pennies to be found and they command a very high selling price. Consider finding one of these coins to be the equivalent of winning a small lottery.

Obverse

Next time you have to choose head or tails in a coin toss, shout OBVERSE. This is the fancy word for heads.

Patina

These are the (pretty or ugly depending on how you look at things) natural colors found in coins made from precious metals that have been exposed to the elements. Silver is more likely to have a natural patina. DO NOT try and remove this natural color. Coins that have a beautiful patina can be worth more money!

Pitted

Small impressions or pits on the surface of a coin. Pitting can be caused by numerous things and it lowers the value of a collectible coin.

Planchet

This is the coin before anything is stuck into the surface. It is a plain metal disc.

Proof

Proof coins are created using a very high quality minting process that produces coins with mirror like or frosted surfaces. The details in these coins are often exaggerated as well. They are made specifically for collecting.

Proof coins are not suppose to make it into circulation, but they do. It is not uncommon to find proof coins when coin roll hunting.

Coin collections get handed down through generations and some people will take them to the bank and turn them into cash not knowing they have Proof coins not meant for circulation.

Reverse

Heads or tails again? How about reverse? This is the back side or tails side of a coin.

Rim

Most coins have two rims. One on the front and one on the back. The rim is the raised portion of a coin that circles the entire diameter of the front or back of a coin. See the image below for an example.

Skunked

A bad day coin roll hunting will have you skunked. This is the term commonly used to refer to not finding anything of value on a coin roll hunting adventure.

Spot Price

This is the up to the minute current price of a precious metal. Precious metal prices can change every few minutes. Spot price was created to help determine a value of a precious metal at the precise time of a sale.

Token

A coin that does not have a monetary value and is not issued by the federal government. Tokens were often used in place of currency. Parking meters, buses and trains used tokens. Private organizations also handed out tokens for marketing purposes.

Tokens are another form of collectible coin. Here is a good token example. I found this token while metal detecting in New Mexico. It was minted somewhere around the late 1800s early 1900s. It was given to patrons of the hotel depicted on the obverse. It was said to bring good luck to anyone holding it. Does it work? I'm not telling!

Toning

Toning is the discoloration found on some coins. At times the toning can have a brilliant rainbow effect. Toning can increase or decrease the value of the coin. It ultimately depends on the buyer. Beauty is in the eye of the beholder. Some people have figured out a way to synthetically create toning using chemicals. This is never a good idea.

Learning the Lingo

There you have it. You have now filled your brain with some coin collecting knowledge that will help you locate coins worthy of your mighty collection, but your education has just begun!

Understanding Mint Marks

See that tiny little D up there I circled? That is the mint mark on a 1943 Mercury Dime. The D means this coin was minted at The Denver Mint. You don't need to have a full understanding of mint marks to have fun finding old coins but mint marks can help you identify a coin with a high value. We will cover that in more detail a little later under the chapter called: What to Look For.

The creation of a coin is referred to as minting. There are different locations or Mints in the United States where coins are made. In order to determine where a coin was minted, they are marked with a small letter that can be difficult to see. That is where the loupe really comes in handy, especially with my eyes.

Not only are mint marks difficult to see at times, but they can also be difficult to find as well. They appear in a different location on every denomination of coin. To make things even more difficult, some coins of the same denomination have mint marks in different locations! You will need a road map just to locate all of the different mint marks!

Mint marks allows the government to keep close tabs on where and how many coins are being minted at each location. It also allows them to track possible errors and stop them from being produced before they end up in the hands of eager collectors.

The lack of a mint mark on a coin is also an indicator of where it was made. Most coins with no mint marks were made at the Philadelphia Mint. There are a few exceptions to this rule.

In 1965, 1966 and 1967 no coins were produced with mint marks. There was a coin shortage during these years and the lack of a mint mark was set in place to discourage the public from collecting coins.

There have been other instances of the government removing mint marks to discourage collecting. This occurred mostly with pennies dated after 1974.

I think you should see a pattern emerging here that has to do with the government always trying to control things, but that is the subject of an entirely different book!

Mint marks can also play a key role in the value of a coin. Some coins may have been produced in small numbers at a specific mint. Any coin that has been produced in limited quantities will have a higher numismatic value to collectors.

Current Mint Marks

Coins that bare a **P** mint mark were minted at The Philadelphia Mint. Remember, some coins with no mint mark were also made at The Philadelphia Mint.

Coins baring a **D** mint mark were minted at The Denver Mint.

Coins baring an **S** mint mark were minted at the San Francisco Mint.

Coins baring a **W** mint mark were minted at the West Point Mint.

At the time of this writing, these were all the active mints currently operating in the United States.

Retired Mint Marks
Even mint marks get the opportunity to retire and relax in South Beach Miami. These mint marks include the following:

Coins baring an **O** mint mark were minted at The New Orleans Mint. This mint produced over 427 million gold and silver coins valued at over 307 million dollars. WOW! I would be happy to own just 2% of those coins!

Coins baring a **CC** mint mark were minted at the Carson City Mint. A lot of gold coins were minted here during its short 19 years of production. Carson City is located in Nevada. A lot of gold has been found in this state. Is that just a coincidence?

Coins baring a **C** mint mark were minted at the Charlotte Mint. This mint was responsible for gold coins. This was also the location of the very first gold mine in the United States. Another coincidence? Not likely.

Early coins baring a **D** mint mark were minted at The Dahlonega Mint. Every single coin minted at this location was made from gold during the years 1838-1861.

Mint marks are not isolated to coins manufactured in the United States. The idea of using mint marks has been around since the ancient times of Greece and Rome and they can be found in coins from all over the world.

Common Errors Types Found While Coin Roll Hunting

The coin manufacturing process is not perfect. In fact, there are mistakes that show up from time to time. Some of these mistakes never make it out of the mint, but there are quite a few that have managed to escape the mint and wind up in circulation.

Some of these coins are considered highly collectible and they can be worth a lot of money. It never hurts to be on the look out for these error coins. I will give you more specific information on which coins have common errors a little later in this book. For now, let's look at the coin errors you can find coin roll hunting.

Brockage
When coins are created, they are supposed to be ejected from the die. This doesn't always happen. Sometimes a coin will stick between the dies and wind up stamping a planchet. The end result is called a brockage. The second coin will have a mirrored image of the first coin that was not properly ejected. See the image below.

Doubled Die

This is often one of the most sought after coin errors. This happens when a coin has an additional misaligned impression on the surface. The error could be very faint and difficult to see, or it could be very obvious like the image below. You can really see the doubling on the date.

Image Credit: Lost Dutchman Rare Coins

Wrong Planchet
This error occurs when the wrong coin denomination is struck on the wrong planchet. For example, a dime being stuck on a planchet designed for a penny. The end result is a coin that looks like a penny in color but has all of the physical characteristics of a dime.

Partial Collar
When coins are created, a collar is used to hold them in

35

place and to apply the design that appears on the edge. A partial collar happens when the collar is not completely lined up when the coin is struck.

Uniface Strike

This happens when two planchets get stuck in the die. As a result, only one side of a coin will have the proper design. The other side is often blank.

Indents

This is yet another coin error when two planchets have been accidentally fed into the die. In this case one the planchets is off center. The end result is a coin with a large blank indention.

Missing Edge Lettering

In 2007, the United States mint started minting gold colored presidential dollar coins. The edges of these coins were supposed to feature the words "In God We Trust" and "E Plurbus Unum." Some of these new coins escaped the mint without the fancy edge lettering or the mint mark.

Filled Die Strike

These are error coins where a portion of the die used the strike the coin became obstructed with something. One of the most notable case of this happening was with the Kansas state quarter. The "T" in the word trust was obstructed with grease. The end result was a quarter that said, "In God We rust."

Common Errors Types Found While Coin Roll Hunting

Coin Grading Scale

The condition of a coin will ultimately determine its numismatic value. A coin that is in better condition will have a higher value than one that is not. Sounds simple enough right? Well it is not quite that easy simply because there are so many variables that come into play when trying to determine the actual condition of a coin.

Some of the points used to grade a coin are valid, while others are simply based on a professional coin graders opinion. Either way, a final grade gets assigned. This final grade will ultimately determine the value of the coin.

Professional Coin Grading Services

There is nothing that says you can't determine the grade of a coin by yourself. In fact,
many private coin collectors do this. It is all part of the hobby, but if you have something that you think is extremely rare or valuable, it is best to have it graded by a professional coin grading service.

Yes this service does cost you a fee, but you get a professional world recognized grading service for the coin in question. The coin is also sealed in a protective container with all the pertinent information appearing somewhere on the protective container. This is done to protect the coin from further damage. Something as simple as the oils from your skin can reduce the value of a coin.

In the United States, you have two options when it comes to having a coin professionally graded.

Numismatic Conservation Service

http://www.ncscoin.com/
Phone: 941.360.3996
email: Service@NCScoin.com

PCGS or Professional Coin Grading Service

http://www.pcgs.com/
United States toll free phone number: 800-447-8848
Outside of the United States phone number: 949-833-0600
Email: info@pcgs.com

Having your coin graded by a professional coin grading service is great and all, but what if you happen to find an old coin at a garage sale that has already been graded? How are you supposed to decipher the grading system and determine the real value of that coin? Be cautious of any coin that has not been graded by a professional. There are plenty of counterfeits out there.

Here are the common coin grading terms and their respective meanings.

We will start with the lowest grade that really isn't worth much, and work our way up to highly sought after higher grades. To the top of the mountain we shall go!

P-1

The **P** in this instance stands for POOR. This is a badly damaged coin that is really only worth its melt value.

FR-2
The **FR** in this instance stands for FAIR. You may be able to see the date and type of coin, but once again the coin is damaged. Good for melt value.

AG-3
Now we are getting somewhere. The **AG** stands for ABOUT GOOD. You should be able to still see the type and date. You should also be able to see some lettering on the coin as well.

G-4
The **G** stands for GOOD. This would be a coin that has heavy wear. It may have little to no numismatic value, unless it is an extremely rare coin.

G-6
As you can see, the numbers in relation to the grading system sort of skip around a little. The **G** stands for good, or GOOD PLUS. This coin would be in slightly better condition than a G-4. It should have a full rim with plenty of good features. It still features heavy wear though.

VG-8
We have now moved from GOOD to VERY GOOD. That is what the letters **VG** stand for in this situation. This coin may still show significant wear, but it will have clearly

discernible features.

F-12
The **F** in this instance stands for the word FINE. This coin will still have moderate wear, but it will also have a distinct rim and clear readable details.

VF-20
The **VF** stands for the words VERY FINE, like my lady. Everything on this coin looks good and clear. The rims are clean and free from nicks. There will be a little wear on lower details and moderate wear on some of the high points.

VF-30
A step up from VF-20. The only difference are the high points are only slightly worn.

EF-40
The **EF** in this instance stands for EXTRA FINE. Everything looks sharp and very clear with wear on the high points.

XF-45
Now we are getting up there in the coin grading world. **XF** stands for EXTRA FINE. Everything in this coin looks clear and crisp. There is very little wear on the high points.

AU-50
The **AU** in this instance stands for ABOUT

UNCIRCULATED. A coin with this grade will have some remaining mint luster and have only a small trace of wear on the higher points.

AU-55
Everything about a coin with this grade is the same as AU-50, but the mint luster must be greater.

AU-58
This coin will appear uncirculated, but can still have very minor wear on the high points.

MS-60 to MS-70
This final portion of the grading scale has some variants. The number used in this grading system can be anywhere from 60 to 70. Coins in this condition are free from any wear. However, they may have dings or bag marks.

Things You May Need

One of the great things about searching for old coins using this method is the fact that you don't really need any special equipment to do it, but that doesn't mean that there are not a few tools out there that will make your hunt for old coins easier. Anyone can do it anytime they feel like it. You can even do this on your lunch hour if you want to. I know quite a few people who do.

Transportation

You will need some form of reliable transportation. You can walk or ride your bike to your local bank. Why not! This is a great way to get some exercise, but if you really want to increase your odds, you will need to cover a lot of ground. That is where some reliable transportation comes in real handy.

Loupe or Magnifying Glass

This may or may not be something you need. Me personally, I need a loupe or a magnifying glass. My eyes just aren't what they use to be.

You can find a jewler's loupe online for around three bucks. If you want to be able to see any tiny imperfections or common coin errors, a loupe or a magnifying glass makes things a lot easier.

Paper Coin Rolls

You can easily remove most coins from their rolls without damaging the roll itself. You could think of this as recycling the roll, but there will be times when you have to tear the paper roll. If you want to redeposit the coins at your local bank, you will need to roll them, unless your bank has a coin sorting machine.

You can find paper coin rolls at just about any major department store, online and at your bank. These will come in really handy.

A Sharpie or A Pen of Some Sort
It is a good idea to mark the rolls you have already searched with some sort of memorable mark. You could draw an X on them. You could put your initials on them, or you could doodle all over the roll. Try to pick something small, yet unique to help you identify rolls you have already searched. This will save you a lot of time.

Metal Detector
Okay, you don't really need a metal detector, but you should own one simply because metal detecting is the best hobby in the world!

A little shameless self promotion coming your way!

I have written several best selling books on the subject that will more than persuade you that metal detecting is the best hobby in the world. You can view them at the following link:

http://www.amazon.com/Mark-D-Smith/e/B00HZ6BM9A/

I have also found a way to use my metal detector to help me sort through coins without even looking at them! I will talk more about this a little later.

Understanding Coin Roll Values

All coins in the United States come in a different size roll with a different monetary value. It helps to understand the total value of each denomination of rolled coin.

Pennies
Pennies come in a roll of 50. You can exchange $1.00 for two rolls of pennies. This would give you a total of 100 coins. You can exchange $10.00 for twenty rolls of pennies or 1000 pennies. This would keep you busy for a while!

Nickels
Nickels come in a roll of 40. They will cost you $2.00 per role.

Dimes
Dimes come in a roll of 50. They will cost you $5.00 per role.

Quarters
Quarters come in a roll of 40. They will cost you $10.00 per roll.

Half Dollars
Half dollars come in a roll of 20. They will cost you $10.00 per roll.

Dollars

There are several dollar coins worth looking for at the bank. The modern presidential dollar coins are the most common. They come in a roll of 25. They will cost you $25.00.

If you happen to come across any larger dollar coins that are rolled, take them all. They very well could be the jackpot. These larger dollar coins come 20 to a roll. They will cost you $20.00.

Setup A Home Base Bank

If you go out coin roll hunting without any sort of plan or method, you will quickly end up with a huge pile of unrolled coins sitting on the floorboards of your car. There is nothing wrong with this, but you will quickly run out of cash and if you happen to visit a bank where you don't have an account, you will not be able to hand them over a pile of unrolled coins. They will politely send you on your way.

The first thing you need to do is setup at least two local bank accounts with a major bank in your area. Think of these banks as your "HOME BASE." The larger the bank in terms of multiple branches, the better. You could also use your own personal bank if you would like.

You don't have to use these banks for any of your personal finances. If you prefer to use a small town community bank or a credit union, then go for it. These banks will be solely used for re-depositing the coins you are not going to keep and turning them back into the cash you will need to buy more coins at the next stop.

You may also want to choose a home based bank that has an automatic sorting machine. If you get heavily into searching for coins, you will need to either roll them all back up or toss them into the sorting machine at your bank. Sorting machines are much easier than spending countless

mind numbing hours trying to roll thousands of coins!

You could even go so far as to open an account at every local bank within a 50 mile radius. That is entirely up to you. I find it easier to keep track of everything with just two bank accounts at competing banks.

Become friends with a few of the tellers at your home base banks. The same goes with the manager. The more people you know at these branches, the better off you will be on your hunt for coins. Knowing any of these people on a first name basis is also very helpful. You are going to be building relationships with these people. They will become your greatest ally!

Once you have become somewhat acquainted with the tellers, mention to them that you are an avid coin collector. Ask them if they can hold any "interesting" coins for you. Also ask them if they can hold any "rolled" coins that other customers may bring into the bank.

As you start to learn which coins bring you the most profit, you can request those specific denominations. For instance, older large dollar coins or any gold "colored" coins that might happen to make a surprise appearance at the bank. You will be surprised by the amount of "interesting" coins that come through the bank on any given day.

Some banks have a zero policy for holding currency for

customers. This does not mean that employees won't do it. Most of them will have no problems doing this for you. Some employees will even be more than happy to call you when "interesting" or "rolled" coins appear. It will ultimately come down to the power of persuasion. I have already talked a little about that.

Some bank employees may catch on that you are looking for rare and valuable coins. They may even decide to keep these coins themselves. This is a very rare occurrence. Most bank employees, especially tellers are there because it is their job. They may or may not like it, but at the end of the day they are there to collect a paycheck.

Planning Your Route

Part of the fun with this hobby is the thrill of the hunt. The excitement of not knowing what you may find on your next stop. You could hit the jackpot, or you could walk away with nothing but a smile on your face. It's all part of the game.

There is nothing that says you have to formally plan a route complete with destination times. Sometimes it never hurts to get behind the wheel of your vehicle and drive down the road with no set destination in mind, only making stops at a bank you happen to pass along the way. This is good old free-rolling free-styling fun. Who knows, you may even pass a great place to break out the metal detector and go for a hunt. What? You still haven't picked one up yet? You don't know what you are missing!

On the other hand, properly planning a coin hunting route can lead to a more productive outing. Knowing exactly where you are going and how many banks and credit unions you will pass along the way can make it easier to fine tune every tiny detail of the adventure ahead.

Planning also helps if you happen to be in an area you are not familiar with. That is one of the really awesome things about this hobby. You don't have to be in any specific location. You could be on vacation in Vail, Colorado. You could be trying to make the most out of your time visiting with the in-laws, or you could be cruising across the country. Your location doesn't matter. In fact, it may even improve your odds.

I like to use a little bit of modern technology when I am in a foreign area and I want to go hunting for coins. You won't believe how easy it is either. You can use an Android based smart phone or a computer with access to the Internet.

If you are using an Android based smart phone, simply open the Google Maps App and type "banks near your location" without the quote marks. For example, if you took the family on vacation to Disney World in Orlando, Florida; you would type banks near Orlando. You can then use the built in GPS features to guide you the entire way. Think of it as having some nagging back seat driver telling you where to go the entire time. Wonderful!

You can do the same thing with a computer minus the GPS features. Open your favorite web browser and go to: maps.google.com. Type in the same search query and Google maps should spit out a handy map with all of the banks within the area. Pretty fancy stuff!

You can do almost the same thing with today's modern GPS devices. Just look for banks and be guided to your next fortune!

Dealing With Bank Tellers

I have already talked about this in previous chapters. A bank teller is either going to be your key to finding untold amounts of treasure, or they are going to be an impenetrable roadblock that is preventing you from reaching your fortune. This is especially true if the teller happens to ask you that one magical question you do not want to hear. "Do you have an account here?"

If the answer is yes, then it will be smooth sailing. If the answer is no, then you might have a problem. Some bank employees don't want to help people who are not account holders. There is a better reply than giving the teller a flat no. You could put a spin on it.

You could say, "No I don't currently have an account here. What do I need to do to open one?" Tellers are always eager to answer this question and it may be all your need to get you foot in the door. Encountering a teller that doesn't want to help you simply because you don't have an account is rare, but it does happen.

Another thing to think about is your appearance. You don't have to be wearing a three piece suit to be successful, but you can't look like a scumbag either. Just try to look somewhat decent before you head off on your coin hunting adventure.

Dealing With Bank Tellers

I have gone coin hunting on my own and with my children. They both really enjoy looking for old coins, but I never expected my children to have such a dramatic impact on the bank tellers. Bank tellers always seemed more eager to help every single time I had my kids with me. This was especially true if I told the teller my children were collecting coins.

One more thing to consider. You will be going in and out of banks looking for various coins. You may even get the bright idea to devise some sort of hand written list that you simply hand to the bank teller. Don't do this. It looks suspicious.

You may also find a bank that has a box of rolled coins that some older customer just brought in. It will be hard to contain your excitement, but you have to keep your wits about you. The trip back to the car with all of those coins will be occupying your mind. Pay attention to what you are doing and where you are going.

One time my son was so eager to get back in our car and start looking through the coins that he accidentally opened the door to a car next to ours and got in the passenger side. He looked over at the driver with a huge smile on his face and then realized he was in the wrong car. That could have ended very badly. What would you do if you just withdrew a large sum of money from your bank account and a complete stranger opened the door to your car and sat right next to you? Pay attention at all times!

Best Times to Go Hunting

Being in the right place at the right time has everything to do with success with this method of coin hunting. You are dealing with odds and pure luck, but there are ways to increase your odds. Knowing the best times to go to the banks can really make a huge difference in your success rate.

Think about your bank for a minute. What are the lobby hours? Most bank lobbies are open Monday – Thursday from 9:00 A.M. Until 4:00 P.M. Good old banker's hours. Most banks will extend their lobby hours by an additional two hours on Friday. Doors are generally open to their customers until 6:00 P.M. Why is this?

A lot of people get paid on Friday. They want to get to the bank and deposit their paychecks in time for the weekend. Whoo hoo! Let's party!

Businesses will also make larger deposits on Friday for pretty much the same reason. A huge influx of deposits happens anytime after 3:00 on Friday at the banks.

This is the single worst time to be there looking for coins. The tellers will be extremely busy dealing with all of the eager depositors. They won't have the time to search for your odd coin requests. Mark Fridays off the calendar.

55

Could any of these Friday deposits contain coins you can add to your collection? You bet they can. That brings you to the best day and time to be at the bank. Some banks are open on Saturday for just a few hours. You could try first thing Saturday morning, but your window of opportunity for this time period is very small. This leaves you with the day of the week most people loathe: Monday.

All the people that might have missed their magical deposit day of Friday will be at the bank first thing Monday morning. Again, this is not a good time to be at the bank. Wait until at least 10:00 and then stroll in with some doughnuts for your favorite teller and a big smile on your face.

Other days to avoid include the 1st of the month, the 15th of the month, the last day of the month and any day before a major bank holiday.

Supply VS Demand

This hobby works on a supply and demand basis. You will ultimately be needing a SUPPLY of cash to exchange for your DEMAND of rolled coins. You will quickly learn that one bank can exhaust your cash supply. This is especially true if you are targeting coins with a larger denomination.

It is not unusual to find banks with hundreds of dollars in rolled coins. There have been several occasions where I have needed in excess of $500.00 just to purchase the bare minimum amount of coins the bank had at that very moment. Don't find yourself shorthanded on cash when you need it the most.

This is why it is important to setup a couple of home base banks where you can resupply your cash flow by depositing all of your unwanted coins.

I recommend playing with at least $500.00 if you are looking for silver halves. If you are looking for copper pennies, then you only need $10-$20.00.

You may be thinking to yourself, "That is a lot of money to be investing in this hobby." You could think of coin hunting as an investment, but by definition the word investment always includes a certain degree of loss. There is NO LOSS with this method of coin hunting.

You are simply moving money from one denomination to another. The only money that does not go back into your bank account exists in the form of valuable collectible coins you find. If anything, you have gained money. If you only paid 50 cents for a silver half dollar that has a melt value of $7.00, how can you lose?

The only possible loss involved in this entire scenario is the cost of gas and that only happens if you choose to go driving all over town. This is not always necessary. Which brings us to our next point.

Ordering Rolled Coins From Your Bank

You do not have to invest a single dime in driving around town looking for valuable coins to add to your collection. Although it can be one of the most productive ways of finding older coins. If you took my advice and setup a couple of home base banks, then you can try ordering rolled coins through the bank.

This is something that many people don't know about simply because they never have a need to order large amounts of coins. Hopefully you created some great relationships with the employees at your home base bank like I suggested. All you need to do is ask for a box of coins in your favorite denomination. If you want to look through nickels, then ask if you can buy a box of nickels.

Most banks do not have a lot of coins handy. With modern technology and the lack of people using cash, banks don't really have that much demand for coins. If the bank teller tells you they do not have any, ask them if they could order a box for you. Expect to spend some serious money hunting for coins this way. The typical price breakdown is as follows.

A box of pennies will cost you $25.00 and keep you busy for months.

A box of nickels will cost you $100.00. That is a total of

2000 nickels you are going to be looking through. You had better get out the coffee for these.

A box of dimes will cost you $250.00.

A box of quarters will cost you $500.00.

A box of half dollars will cost you $500.00.

As you can see, ordering rolled coins from the bank will more than satisfy your urge to hunt for valuable coins.

Which Coins Will Produce the Best Results?

The answer to this question really depends on what your intended outcome is. You may be looking for silver coins. You may be looking to fill a hole in your state quarter collection, or you may be interested in keeping pennies for their copper content. Determining what you want will make it easier to determine which coins you should be searching through.

You may be saying, "I want to find all the valuable coins!" Me too, and you can easily target multiple denominations to add to your collection. Here is a breakdown that will make things a little easier for you.

Gold Hunters
Everyone wants to find a gold coin. The odds of finding one are very slim, but it does happen from time to time. Your best bet for finding any gold coins is by looking through modern presidential dollars and rolled quarters. These are the two places where someone will most likely make a mistake and deposit a gold coin.

Silver Hunters
Your chances of finding silver while coin hunting are good. They are very good if you know what to look for. I will talk more about that a little later. If you are hunting for silver, then target these coins in this order.

Which Coins Will Produce the Best Results?

- Old larger dollars
- Half dollars
- Nickels
- Dimes
- Quarters

If you are trying to fill a hole in your collection, then you should already know what to look for.

What To Look For

This is where your coin hunting education is going to be kicked into high gear. This is where you are going to learn exactly which coins under each denomination are worth keeping. This is the meat and potatoes of the plan. I hope you are hungry because there is a lot to eat.

Half Dollars

Let's start this addictive hobby on the right foot. Let's start by targeting coins that will most likely produce results in a short amount of time. No one likes to invest any amount of time into a hobby and in return get little to nothing out of it. If this is your first time hunting for coins at the bank, then you need to start with the half dollar. Here is what you need to look for.

Take any half dollar you can find. I don't care if it is a single half dollar, or an entire $500 box worth. Take every single one you can find and look for the following. Any of these are worth keeping regardless of their condition.

Seated Liberty Half Dollar 1840-1873

Image Credit: Lost Dutchman Rare Coins

Extremely rare! These are 90% silver but they have an extremely high numismatic value due to their rarity. Look for the rare and elusive 1877 CC seated liberty half dollar.

Barber Half Dollars 1892-1915

Image Credit: Lost Dutchman Rare Coins

These are very difficult to find. They are 90% silver, but due to their age these coins have a high numismatic value. If you do happen to find one of these rare coins, here are the most valuable.

1892 O Mint Mark

1982 S Mint Mark
1983 S Mint Mark
1897 O Mint Mark
1897 S Mint Mark
1904 S Mint Mark
1914

Walking Liberty Half Dollar 1916-1947

Image Credit: Brandon Grossardt

These show up every once in a while. They are 90% silver and depending on their condition can have a high numismatic value as well. Keep them all and look out for these.

1916 S Mint Mark
1917 O Mint Mark Obverse
1919 D Mint Mark
1921
1921 D Mint Mark
1921 S Mint Mark

Ben Franklin Half Dollar 1948-1964

Image Credit: John Baumgart

These can also make an appearance. They are 90% silver and they can have a high numismatic value as well.

Kennedy Half Dollar 1964

This is your only chance at finding a Kennedy half dollar that contains 90% silver.

Kennedy Half Dollar 1965-1970
These coins are also worth more than their 50 cent face value because they are 40% silver. The likely hood of finding these is even greater!

Kennedy Half Dollar 1976 S Mint Mark
These coins are made from 40% silver.

Kennedy Half Dollar 1974 D Mint Mark Doubled Die Obverse
This coin has a high numismatic value because it appears as if the letters are doubled.

Other Kennedy Half Dollars Worth Collecting
1995 S Silver Proof
1998 S Silver Proof
1971 D and 1977 D struck on 40% silver
1979 S Proof Filled S and Clear S
1981 S Proof Clear S and Flat S

Pennies

Pennies are one of the best places to start simply because you can get so many of them for such a small amount of money. I didn't include them first because most pennies you find will not have as high of a monetary value as the Half dollars due to their silver content. Here are the pennies you need to keep your eyes open for.

Indian Head Penny 1859-1909

These are collectible for both the copper content and the age.

Wheat Penny 1909-1958

These are collectible for both the copper content and the age. There are a few wheat pennies worth collecting. Keep your eyes open for these.

1909 S VDB
1909 S Mint Mark over Horizontal S
1909 S Mint Mark
1914 D Mint Mark
1917 Double Die Obverse
1922 Plain Wheat Penny – This penny was minted in Denver, but has no mint mark. These are a great find and very valuable.
1931 S Mint Mark
1936 Double Die Obverse
1941 Double Die

1942 S Mint Mark Double Die
1943 D Double Mint Mark
1943 Bronze Penny
1944 D Mint Mark over S
1946 S Mint Mark over D
1951 D S Mint Mark double mint mark
1952 D S Mint Mark double mint mark
1956 D S Mint Mark double mint mark
1955 Double Die Obverse
1958 Double Die Obverse

1943 S Steel Penny

During World War II, the United States was facing a copper shortage due to the demand of ammunition. During the year 1943, no pennies were made from copper. They were all made from steel. It is easy to spot one of these pennies because they are silver in color. This is a rare coin that fits perfectly in any collection.

Lincoln Penny 1959-1981

The chances of you finding one of these pennies is very good. There is a good chance you have a few sitting around the house right now. Why would you want to keep these? That is a good question.

People always say history repeats itself. When coins were originally being created from silver, the silver content was not worth more than the face value of the coin. Look at the price of silver now. It has gone through the roof. Very few people had the insight to collect silver coins way back in the day, but the ones who did were able to turn a huge profit.

Lincoln cents made from 1959-1982 are made from 95% copper. History has taught us that the value of certain metals increases over time. Any Lincoln penny made from 1959-1982 is now worth more in copper than the face value of the coin. If history does in fact repeat itself, then collecting as many of these pennies as you can might be a really good idea. It's not like it will set you back much. We are talking pennies here.

Going through a mountain of pennies looking for these specific dates can be a huge pain in the rear, but I found an easier way to do it. I use my metal detector to tell me what the penny is made from.

I have my metal detector setup in such a way that copper pennies make a different sound than modern zinc pennies. I can quickly wave a penny in front of the search coil and instantly know whether it is copper or zinc.

With this advanced method, I can go through an entire roll of pennies in about a minute and separate the copper from the zinc. My son now has a healthy collection of these pennies that one day could very well be worth a small fortune!

Here are some other Lincoln pennies to be on the look out for.

1960 Double D Mint Mark
1964 Double Die
1969 S Mint Mark Double Date
1969 S Mint Mark Double Die
1970 S Mint Mark Double Die Obverse
1971 S Mint Mark Double Die Obverse
1980 Double Die
1982 Double Die
1983 Doubling One Cent on Reverse
1984 Double Ear Lobe
1995 Double Liberty

Nickels

Nickels are another great denomination where you have a good chance of finding some silver coins. Yes, the United States Mint did make nickels from silver. How ironic. Another great reason to look through nickels is the low cost involved. Here is what you need to keep your eyes open for when searching through nickels.

Liberty or V Nickel 1883-1912

Any Liberty Head nickel is worth keeping for the numismatic value alone.

Buffalo Nickel 1913-1938

It is not uncommon to find Buffalo Head nickels at the bank. You should keep them all based on the numismatic value alone, but there are a few really special ones to keep your eyes open for. Here they are.

1913 S Type 1 – The Buffalo appears to be standing on a hill of grass and the words FIVE CENTS appear on the mound of grass.

1913 S Type 2 – The hill of grass is cut off and the words FIVE CENTS appear on a small flat area of the coin just like the coin in the image above.

1916 Double Die

1918 D Mint Mark Double Die 8 Over 7
1921 S Mint Mark
1924 S Mint Mark
1926 S Mint Mark
1937 D Mint Mark Three Legged Buffalo

Jefferson War Nickel 1942-1945

Image Credit Bobby131313

This nickel is known as the Silver War Time Nickel. It consists of 35% silver. Great addition to your silver collection.

Here are some other Jefferson nickels to be on the look out for.

1939 D Mint Mark
1943 P Doubled Die Obverse
1949 D - D over S Mint Mark
1950 D Mint Mark
1954 S – S over D Mint Mark
1955 D – D over S Mint Mark
1968 No Mint Mark
1969 No Mint Mark
1970 No Mint Mark
1990 D No Designer Initials
2005 D Speared Bison Nickel – A die problem created a line the goes through the bison. It appears as if the bison was speared.

Dimes

Dimes are also another great place to find those valuable silver coins. Plus you don't need to spend a fortune to get a few rolls. Searching through dimes can be tough on older eyes. This is when a good loupe or magnifying glass comes in real handy. Here are the coins to look for.

Seated Liberty Dime 1837-1891

Any seated liberty dime is worth keeping based on the numismatic value in addition to the silver content.

Barber Dime 1892-1916

Any Barber dime is worth keeping based on the numismatic value in addition to the silver content.

Winged Liberty Head Mercury Dime 1916-1945

This is one of my favorite coins. I don't know why. It just is. While finding one of these at the bank is rare, it is not impossible. I have found a few of them. They are worth keeping based on the numismatic value in addition to the silver content. Keep your eyes open for these high value mercury dimes.

1916 D Mint Mark
1921
1921 D Mint Mark
1926 S Mint Mark
1931 S Mint Mark
1942 1 Over 2 Date Error

Roosevelt Dime 1946-1964 Roosevelt Dime

These coins are 90% silver. Consider them to be keepers!

Roosevelt Dime 1965 to Present
These coins do not contain silver, but there are a few worth hunting for. Keep your eyes open for these.

1982 No P Mint Mark
1996 W Mint Mark

Presidential Dollars

These are the newer gold colored dollar coins that depict a variety of presidents. You won't be able to find any coins made from precious metals by searching through newer presidential dollars, but there are some error coins that are worth keeping simply for the numismatic value. All of these coins are supposed to have lettering and mint marks on the edge of the coin. The valuable ones have errors in this area. Here are the ones to look for.

2007 Washington Missing Edge Lettering
2007 John Adams Missing Edge Lettering
2007 P Mint Mark John Adams Double Edge Lettering

Quarters

Quarters are definitely worth looking through. You do have the chance of finding some silver coins, but it is rare. There are some other interesting quarters worth looking for as well.

Seated Liberty Quarter 1838-1891

Any seated liberty quarter is worth keeping based on the numismatic value in addition to the silver content. If you are lucky enough to find any of these, keep your eyes open for the following.

1870 CC Mint Mark
1871 CC Mint Mark
1872 S Mint Mark
1873 CC Mint Mark with Arrows

Barber Quarter 1892-1916

Any barber quarter is worth keeping based on the numismatic value in addition to the silver content. If you are lucky enough to find any of these, keep your eyes open for the following.

1892 S Mint Mark
1893 S Mint Mark
1895 S Mint Mark

Barber Quarter 1892-1916

1896 O Mint Mark
1896 S Mint Mark
1897 O Mint Mark
1897 S Mint Mark
1901 O Mint Mark
1901 S Mint Mark
1913 S Mint Mark
1914 S Mint Mark

Standing Liberty Quarter 1916-1930

Any standing liberty quarter is worth keeping based on the numismatic value in addition to the silver content. If you are lucky enough to find any of these, keep your eyes open for the following.

1916
1918 S 18 Over 17 Doubled Die Obverse
1919 D Mint Mark
1919 S Mint Mark
1921
1923 S Mint Mark

Washington Quarter 1932-1964

Any 1932-1964 Washington quarter is worth keeping based on the numismatic value in addition to the silver content. If you are lucky enough to find any of these, keep your eyes open for the following.

1932 D Mint Mark
1932 S Mint Mark
1934 Light Motto

1934 Heavy Motto
1934 Doubled Die Obverse In God We Trust
1937 Doubled Die Obverse In God We Trust
1942 D Mint Mark Doubled Die Obverse In God Liberty
1943 Doubled Die Obverse In God We Trust
1943 S Mint Mark Doubled Die Obverse In God We Trust
1950 D Mint Mark D Over S
1950 S Mint Mark S Over D

Washington Quarter 1965-Present
Only one of these coins will contain silver, but there are a few worth hunting for. Keep your eyes open for these.

1976 S Mint Mark 40% Silver
1983 P Mint Mark Uncirculated

Washington State Quarters 1999-2008
These can be fun to collect for the sole purpose of having a complete set. There are a few error coins worth looking for.

2004 D Mint Mark Extra Leaf High
2004 D Mint Mark Extra Leaf Low
2005 P Mint Mark In God We Rust

Large Dollar Coins

If you happen to walk into a bank and ask for dollar coins and their reply is, "We only have the larger old ones." TAKE THEM ALL! There is a really good chance these may be some high value coins! Here is what you need to look for.

Seated Liberty Dollar 1836-1873

Image Credit: Lost Dutchman Rare Coins

Any seated liberty dollar is worth keeping based on the numismatic value in addition to the silver content. If you are lucky enough to find any of these, keep your eyes open for the following.

1850
1851
1851 O Mint Mark
1852
1854
1855
1856
1857
1861
1862
1870 CC Mint Mark
1870 S Mint Mark
1871 CC Mint Mark
1872 CC Mint Mark
1873 CC Mint Mark
1873 S Mint Mark

Morgan Dollar 1878-1904 1921

Image Credit: Brandon Grossardt

Any Morgan dollar is worth keeping based on the numismatic value in addition to the silver content. If you are lucky enough to find any of these keep your eyes open for the following.

1881 CC Mint Mark
1885 CC Mint Mark

1889 CC Mint Mark
1893 CC Mint Mark
1893 S Mint Mark
1895 Proof
1895 S Mint Mark

Peace Dollar 1921-1935 1964

Any Peace dollar is worth keeping based on the numismatic value in addition to the silver content. If you are lucky enough to find any of these, keep your eyes open for the following.

1921
1928
1934 D Doubled Die
1934 S Mint Mark Uncirculated

Eisenhower Dollar 1971-1978

Any of these coins are worth collecting simply because they are no longer being made. There are a few which are made from 40% silver and there are a few other varieties worth looking for. Keep your eyes open for these.

One of the more interesting coins to look for is the 1972. During this year, the coin had 3 different back designs. They have been labeled "Type 1" "Type 2" and "Type 3".

Use the images below to help you get a better understanding of the differences. Type 2 commands the highest value.

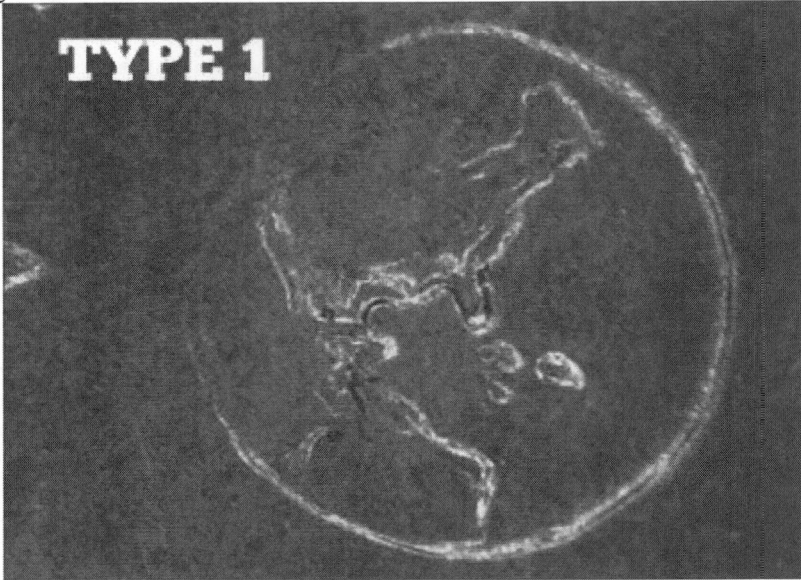

Eisenhower Dollar 1971-1978

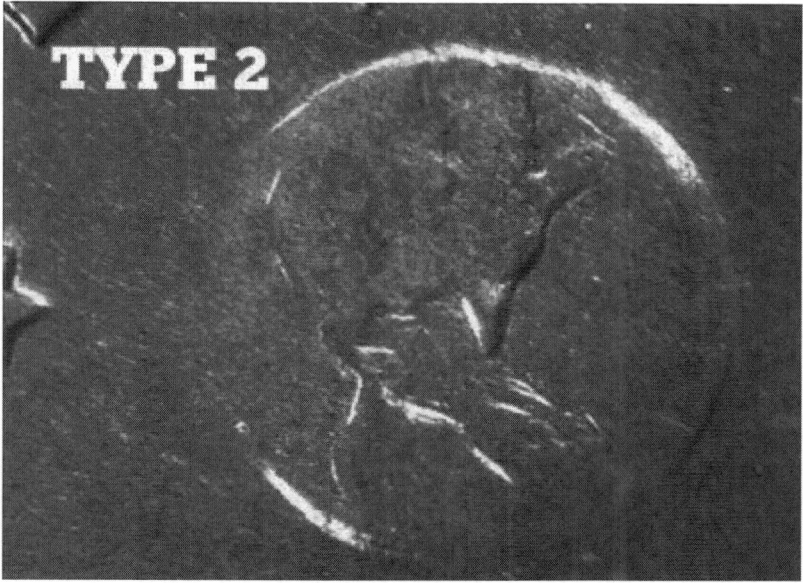

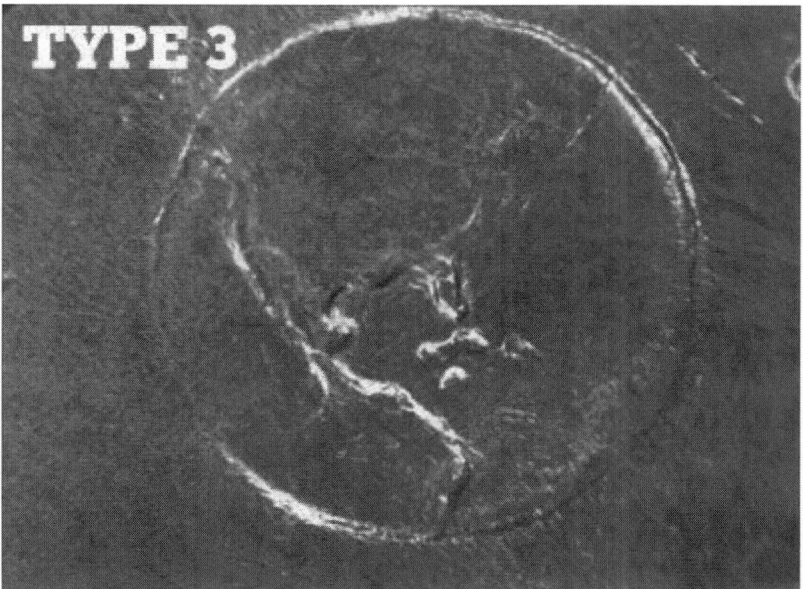

Image credits: The Ike Group
Other notable Eisenhower dollars

1971 S Mint Mark 40% Silver
1972 Type 2
1973 S Mint Mark 40% Silver
1974 S Mint Mark 40% Silver
1976 S Mint Mark 40% Silver

Other Notable Dollar Coins

There are plenty of other notable dollar coins worth looking for as well.

Susan B Anthony Dollar 1979-1981 1999

1979 P Mint Mark Wide Rim Near Date

Sacagawea Dollar 2000-Present

2000 P Mint Mark Cheerios – There are extra feathers that appear on the tale of the eagle right behind the talons. The regular variety has no feather detail here.

2000 P Wounded Eagle – An arrow goes through the eagle's body.

Other Places to Find Old Coins

Banks are not the only place where you will have luck finding old coins. I have had the best luck finding old coins using my metal detector. The sheer amount of valuable coins buried right beneath our feet is mind boggling. If you have ever thought about metal detecting, check out my best selling book called

<u>Metal Detecting: A Beginner's Guide to Mastering the Greatest Hobby In the World.</u>

This book shows the Ins and Outs of the hobby in great detail. It is well worth the read.

There are plenty of other great places to find old coins without a metal detector. You may even have some in the change jingling around in your pocket. Here are some other great places to look for old coins.

- Old Coin Jars
- Piggy Banks
- Casinos
- Garage Sales
- Thrift Shops
- Coin Sorting Machines
- Store Clerks
- Coin shows
- Coin Dealers
- Laundromats

- Grocery Stores
- Department Stores

With a little bit of creative thinking, you may be able to add to this list of great places to locate old coins.

Cleaning Your Finds

To clean, or not to clean. That is the question! There are some situations where cleaning your finds just might destroy the value. If there is any doubt in your mind, then you probably should not be cleaning your new piece of treasure. This is especially true with old coins that have a nice natural patina. They are far more valuable in their current state than if you cleaned them.

There will also be times when you will want to clean an item in order to properly display it or sell it. Here are some of the best methods for cleaning some of the great coins you are going to be finding.

Cleaning Clad Coins

Over a period of time, you will wind up with a lot of clad coins. You may even want to take them all to the bank and deposit them. Cleaning clad is fairly easy because you don't have to worry about doing any damage to these coins. Their only monetary value is their current face value.

A rock tumbler is an excellent way to give these types of coins a good cleaning. If you don't have a rock tumbler, then there are a few other great ways to clean the mountain of clad coins you have been finding.

I use an old plastic fruit juice jug. I put some sand, and a mixture of vinegar and water in the juice jug along with all the coins and give it a good shaking. Then I empty all the coins into an old colander and rinse them with fresh water. This is usually good enough for the bank.

Cleaning Valuable Coins

The value of older coins is based on a few things. The amount of like coins that were minted, and the current condition of the coin. If you happen to damage the coin while you attempt to clean it, then you could be making a huge mistake.

If you have an older coin that you want cleaned, then you had better leave this up to the professionals. There are professional coin cleaning and grading services out there. The two most popular are:

Numismatic Conservation Service
http://www.ncscoin.com/
Phone: 941.360.3996
Email: Service@NCScoin.com

PCGS or Professional Coin Grading Service
http://www.pcgs.com/
United States toll free phone number: 800-447-8848
Outside of the United States phone number: 949-833-0600
Email: info@pcgs.com

If you have an older coin that is not extremely valuable

and you want to clean it up yourself, there are a few proven methods that work quite well.

The Slow Coin Cleaning Method

If you don't mind waiting a little while (sometimes 2-3 months), then soak your coin in olive oil. This method has proven to clean even the most stubborn dirty coin with no visible damage. The down side is that this method can take a very long time. If you can wait, stick to this method. If you can't wait, then try some of these other great cleaning methods.

Faster Coin Cleaning Options

Toothpaste works wonders on old tarnished metals. Work a small dab of toothpaste onto the surface of the coin using your fingers. You can also use a soft bristled toothbrush to help loosen up some of the crud on the coin. Rinse and repeat until the coin looks good.

Another neat trick involves a little bit of science. Rub the old coin with a wet piece of tinfoil. This creates a mild electrolysis effect and cleans the surface of the coin.

Some people have also had great results cleaning coins using baking soda, vinegar and lemon juice. They can all be used separately, or in some type of crazy mad scientist concoction. Just be careful if you plan on mixing chemicals. You could be asking for all sorts of problems.

What Should You Do With Your Coins?

Now that you have collected a heaping pile of valuable coins, you might be wondering what you should do with them? I keep all of my coins in hopes of one day achieving total world domination. You may want to keep all of your coins and hand them down to your children when the time is right.

You are really only faced with two options. You can keep all of the coins you worked so hard to find and try to achieve world domination like myself, or you can turn them into cold hard cash and blaze a trail across the United States that makes the book Fear and Loathing In Las Vegas look like a children's novel.

Protecting Your Coins

If you have opted to keep your mountain of coins, then you will need to find some way to protect them. Believe it or not there are right ways and wrong ways to go about doing this. In order to determine the best ways to protect your valuable coins, I am going to turn this portion of the book over to a dear friend of mine, Professor James Vaughn Stinkles. (Of course I am kidding here, but just follow along. It might make things more interesting. You may even want to read this next part in a scientific scholar like voice.) Take it away Mr. Stinkles.

Coins that exhibit a high numismatic value should be properly cared for in order to retain their maximum value. The most common mistake in which the amateur coin collector makes is handling the coins using nothing more than their bare hands. This should be considered a faux pas.

You see, the oils in our skin can cause irreversible damage to the surface of a coin. Any coins with a high numismatic value should only be handled using a white velvet glove.

Okay enough of Mr. Stinkles. If you have any really valuable coins, don't handle them with your bare hands. If you must handle your coins, don't rub the surface with your finger. Only hold your coins by the edge. Pretty simple, but there are other things that can cause problems for your coin collection as well.

Humidity Is Bad!

If you happen to live in the deep south where on any given day the humidity is well over 100%, then you will have problems. Water in even the smallest form can and will hurt your coin collection. Silver and copper will change color if exposed to water even if it is in the form of excess humidity.

In some cases avoiding humidity is pretty much impossible. What is the best way to protect a valuable coin from these problems? It really depends on the coin's value.

For instance, if you are keeping copper pennies simply for the copper, then you can throw them into a five gallon bucket if you want. The actual condition of the coin doesn't matter. It is the copper you are after. The same could be said of silver coins that have no numismatic value.

Now if you happen to have a nice collection of proofs or some type of old coin that has a high numismatic value, you are better off keeping them in a sealed, protective coin container. Again, the value of the coin should dictate the container. Extremely rare coins should be professionally graded and sealed by a professional coin grading company. Semi valuable coins can be stored in protective, plastic coin containers you can find on the Internet.

Storing Your Coins

Now that you know how to offer your coins the greatest form of protection, you need to find a place for them. The first place many people think of is a safety deposit box at the bank. I would advise against this. Banks may not always hold your best interests at heart. If the economy should take a serious nose dive, would your coins be safe at the bank? Many people, including myself don't think so. The government could easily come in and take everything.

Banks are also closed during all natural disasters. A closed bank means no access to your coins.

Many people also have the false impression that the contents of their safety deposit box are insured. This is not true. The contents of a safety deposit box are not insured. What would happen to your coins if an earthquake, tornado, hurricane or flood washed your bank away. Bye bye coins!

Storing coins or any large amounts of precious metals at your home is also dangerous, especially if you are being watched. I know it sounds like I am being paranoid here, but I am not. Thieves have broken into people's houses and stolen all of their precious metals because the thieves knew they were there.

You may get the bright idea to store all of your valuable

coins in a PVC tube and bury them in the backyard. PVC will damage your coins! Don't do this.

The burying part sounds like a good idea too, but what if your neighbor is watching you? A metal detector is all it takes to locate your buried stash. There are ways to safely bury coins so that no one with a metal detector will find them, but it takes a ton of work to do this.

You will need to dig at least four feet down and then scatter a bucket full of nails throughout the dirt as you shovel all the earth back in the hole. You might as well litter your entire back yard with nothing but nails if you want to keep the best detectorists from locating your stash in the middle of the night.

One great option is to use a safe, and you had better use a really good one that does not use a key. A combination safe is the way to go and only share the combination with one other person.

What if a thief finds your safe? That is where a decoy safe comes into play. Buy a cheap safe from the local office supply store and put a few junker coins and some costume jewelry inside. Keep it on the top shelf of your closet in plain site. If a thief does break into your home, they will find the decoy safe first and be happy to take it. You may even want to have some fun with this one.

Buy some gold spray paint and a bunch of lead. Spend the

afternoon spray painting all the lead. Toss that in the cheap safe and the thieves will think they have hit it big time!

If you don't like the idea of using a safe, you can look for a company that offers private vault storage. This concept has not hit the mainstream yet, but it is catching on and finding private vault storage is becoming easier with every passing day.

Selling Your Collection

If you don't plan on keeping your coins, then the only other obvious choice would be to sell them. The first place many people go is the good old pawn shop down the street. Don't do this. Sorry pawn shop owners. I know you need to make a buck too. Pawn shops will pay you for your coins, but they will not pay you for the full value. Your best bet is to sell them direct and there are several ways you can do this.

Locate A Reputable Coin Dealer

Not all coin dealers are the same. Some of them are worse than pawn shops. If you plan on taking some coins to your local coin dealer in hopes of selling them, do a little research first to see what those coins are selling for. All it takes is a quick search on the Internet to figure out how much a coin is worth, but that does not mean the coin dealer will pay this price. You will need to barter with them to get a price close to the current value of the coin.

If you like collecting coins, visiting a coin dealer will blow your mind. They will have some of the best coins you have ever seen. You may end up leaving the shop with a pocket full of new coins.

Coin dealers are also usually open to trade. If you have several coins that you don't want, ask the dealer if they will trade you for a few coins you may need. I have never met a coin dealer who was not open to trading.

113

Selling Your Collection Online

Yes you can sell all of your collection or just pieces of it through some of the various online auction sites. There are plenty of people who do this and they make some serious money. That means you can too!

The Smithsonian Institution

If you really find yourself enjoying coin collecting, then you must plan at least one trip to the Smithsonian Institution and feast your eyes on The National Numismatic Collection. You might want to bring a change of pants too because this is one coin collection that might make you lose control of your bodily functions.

This collection includes over 450,000 coins and over 1.1 million pieces of paper money. The collection also boasts some of the rarest coins on the planet including one of only three known to exist 1933 Double Eagles. The collection is unbelievable.

You don't have to go all the way to Washington D.C. To see the collection. You can view it online by clicking here:

The National Numismatic Collection

As soon as you are done drooling over this impressive collection, plan a visit. It will take a few days to see everything with your own eyes.

Smithsonian Institute
1000 Jefferson Dr SW
Washington D.C. 20004
202-633-1000
www.si.edu

Join the Coin Collecting Community

Just like you, there are plenty of other people out there who love to not only collect coins, but to talk about their experiences and share their wealth of knowledge. Luckily, there are plenty of places where all of us can get together and exchange information in regards to collecting coins.

If you want to reach out and connect with other people, then you have a couple of great choices. If you like the idea of actually meeting people face to face to talk about collectible coins, then joining a local coin club will be your best bet. There are coin clubs all over the United States. All you need to do is search for the words "coin club" on the Internet. You will get plenty of results. If you add the name of a major city close to your home in the search, then you can really narrow down a good local coin club.

For instance: if you live in or near Chicago, search for "Chicago coin club" without the quotes.

Coin clubs are a great way to meet with other people who also love collecting coins. Many members get together to show off their collections. You may also get a chance to see some very rare coins!

Online Communities

If you can't seem to find a local club, then you are still in luck. There are several great online coin collecting

116

communities out there where thousands of eager coin collectors meet every single day from all over the world to share their finds, tips and advice. This can be a great way to learn about the value of coins from other parts of the world as well.

The amount of information that can be found and learned from these online communities is invaluable, and you don't even have to take part in any of the online conversations if you don't feel like it. You can sit on the sidelines and watch and read everything quietly.

I do have a word of warning though. You might want to think about it before you post your greatest find on a public forum. It is a great feeling to share your finds with others, but over a period of time you may wind up posting quite a few great finds. Now anyone who browses these forums can see just how many valuable coins you may have in your possession. This kind of information can be dangerous if it falls into the wrong hands.

Now don't take this the wrong way. There are always a few bad apples in the bunch. Just be careful about what you post and how frequently you are doing it.

Here are some great online coin collecting communities worth checking out.
http://www.coincommunity.com/forum/

https://www.cointalk.com/forums/

http://www.coinpeople.com/

http://boards.collectors-society.com/ubbthreads.php?
ubb=cfrm&c=4

http://www.pcgs.com/messageboards.html

Additional Resources

Coin collecting is a hobby that is always evolving. New coins are produced each year and with each round of production there is always the possibility of new errors. Being one of the first people to know about these errors definitely gives you an upper hand when it comes to collecting them. Being part of the community is a great place to start, but there are plenty of other places where you can increase your coin collecting knowledge.

The US Mint

The US Mint is the place to learn about any new coins that are scheduled for release. There are also times when The US Mint will create limited runs of coins that can be very valuable to collectors all over the world. Their website is the best way to keep your finger on the pulse of newly minted coins.

http://www.usmint.gov/

Coin Books

I would love to say that this book is the only one you need to successfully find and collect rare and valuable coins, but it is far from it. This book is meant to inform you about the valuable coins that may be sitting in the vault of your local bank or your grandparents sock drawer.

As you get deeper into the hobby of collecting coins, you will obviously require more knowledge on the subject.

Additional Resources

There are plenty of great books out there worth purchasing or borrowing from your local library. Here are some names as well as links to some other coin collecting books you might want to consider.

The Official Red Book
http://www.amazon.com/Guide-Book-United-States-Coins-ebook/dp/B00JT0M1OK/

This is "the" book when it comes to collecting coins from the United States. It is a yearly publication, but that does not mean you need to purchase a copy each year.

Handbook of United States Coins
http://www.amazon.com/Handbook-United-States-Coins-2014-ebook/dp/B00DP8OD8O/

Yet another fantastic book for collecting coins from the United States.

World Coin Books
At one point in time every single coin collector will reach out and start taking an interest in coins from other countries. There are several great books on this subject as well. World coin books cover very specific date ranges. If you purchase any of these books, pay close attention to the dates covered in each book. World coin books can be a little on the pricey side because they have so much information in them.

2015 Standard Catalog of World Coins 2001-Date
http://www.amazon.com/Standard-Catalog-World-Coins-2001-Date/dp/144024040X/

Collecting World Coins 1901-Present
http://www.amazon.com/Collecting-World-Coins-1901-Present-George/dp/1440236186/

Standard Catalog of World Coins – 1801-1900
http://www.amazon.com/Standard-Catalog-World-Coins-1801-1900/dp/1440230854/

2015 Standard Catalog of World Coins 1901-2000
http://www.amazon.com/Standard-Catalog-World-Coins-1901-2000/dp/1440240396/

Above all else. Have fun! Coin collecting of any kind, including coin roll hunting is supposed to be a thrilling hobby where you never really know what you may find. Don't let a few rolls of skunks prevent you from having a good time out there. It happens to all of us. It is all just a matter of being in the right place at the right time.

Thanks!

If you enjoyed Coin Hunting Made Easy, then click here to leave a review! I would really appreciate it.

You may also be interested in some of my other books below. There is treasure to be found everywhere.

Incredible Metal Detecting Discoveries: True Stories of Amazing Treasures Found by Everyday People

This book showcases the best treasures unearthed using nothing more than a metal detector. Each true story of amazing treasure discoveries will have you itching to get out there and find your very own piece of treasure. From monster gold nuggets worth millions of dollars to ancient buried hoards that consist of thousands of gold coins, the stories in this book will take your breath away!

Click here to Pick up a copy in the Amazon Kindle Store.

If you want to learn what it is like to metal detect at the beach and uncover loads of treasure, take a look at my best selling book entitled:

Metal Detecting the Beach

It is packed full of great beach hunting tips, tricks and

Thanks!

secrets. It is available in digital format and paperback.

The greatest tip that I can leave you with is this. Persistence pays. You never know when you will find that next great piece of treasure. Believe me, it is out there and it is waiting for you to discover it! Get out there and have fun.

Printed in Great Britain
by Amazon.co.uk, Ltd.,
Marston Gate.